J 306.850971 For

Foran, J.
Family life.

PRICE: $22.95 (3582/01   )

W9-CHG-862

Family Life

by Jill Foran

WEIGL EDUCATIONAL PUBLISHERS

TOWN OF CALEDON PUBLIC LIBRARY

Published by Weigl Educational Publishers Limited
6325-10 Street SE
Calgary, Alberta
Canada T2H 2Z9
Web site: www.weigl.com

Copyright 2004 WEIGL EDUCATIONAL PUBLISHERS LIMITED
All rights reserved. No part of this publication may be reproduced, stored in
a retrieval system, or transmitted in any form or by any means, electronic,
mechanical, photocopying, recording, or otherwise, without the prior written
permission of Weigl Educational Publishers Limited.

Canadian Cataloguing in Publication Data
Foran, Jill
        Family life / Jill Foran.

(Early Canadian life)
Includes index.
ISBN 1-55388-041-2 (lib. bound: alk. paper)
ISBN 1-55388-057-9 (pbk.)

        1. Family--Canada--History--Juvenile literature.
2. Frontier and pioneer life--Canada--Juvenile literature. I. Title. II. Series:
Early Canadian life (Calgary, Alta.)

FC85.F67 2003   j306.85'0971   C2003-905430-6

Printed and bound in the United States of America
1 2 3 4 5 6 7 8 9 0 06 05 04 03

We acknowledge the
financial support of the
Government of Canada
through the Book
Publishing Industry
Development Program
(BPIDP) for our
publishing activities.

Photograph Credits
Every reasonable effort has been made to trace
ownership and to obtain permission to reprint
copyright material. The publishers would be
pleased to have any errors or omissions brought
to their attention so that they may be corrected
in subsequent printings.

Ellen Bryan: 15T; **Glenbow Archives:** pages 1
(NA-2583-8), 4 (NA-2384-1), 7 (NA-3961-14), 9
(NA-1941-12), 23R (NA-2695-1); **Fred Hultstrand
History in Pictures Collection NDIRS-NDSU, Fargo:**
page 17 (2028.261); **Minnesota Pioneer Park:** pages
8, 11; **National Archives of Canada:** pages 3B (John
Boyd/RD-000057), 5 (Edward Roper/C-011030), 6
(Alexander Henderson/PA-181769), 10 (PA-117285),
14T (Edward Roper/C-0013884), 14B (William George
Richardson Hind/C-103003), 15B (Henry Buckton
Laurence/C-041083), 18 (John Boyd/
RD-000057), 23L (Philip J. Bainbrigge/C-011811);
photocanada.com: page 12; **photos.com:** page 20;
Courtesy of Rogers Communications Inc: page 22;
Tina Schwartzenberger: pages 3T, 13T, 13B, 19.

Project Coordinator
Tina Schwartzenberger

Design
Janine Vangool

Layout
Bryan Pezzi

Copy Editor
Janice L. Redlin

Photo Researcher
Ellen Bryan

Contents

Introduction

Imagine having chores to do all day long. When pioneers first settled in Canada, they had to work from sunrise to sunset. In the 1700s and 1800s, pioneer families came to Canada from Europe and the United States. Their lives in Canada were not easy. It took many years of hard work for families to live comfortably.

On the prairies where there were few trees, families built homes with blocks of grass and earth called sod. The Aitkenhead family built their sod house near Naseby, Saskatchewan.

In order to keep their homestead or farm, pioneer families had to build a house and grow crops on a certain amount of land each year. If they did this for 3 years, the family could keep the land.

In early Canada, almost all pioneer families had a farm or **homestead**. After arriving in their new country, a family started to develop their farm. Often, the family had travelled to Canada with very few belongings. The whole family had responsibilities. Together, the father, mother, and children worked to create a productive farm and household. Everyone had many jobs to do.

Did you know:

In Canada's early days, a pioneer family's house was often a one-room cabin. Inside this cabin, the family ate, cooked, did household chores, and slept.

A Father's Work

In most pioneer families, the father was the head of the household. He made important decisions. The father chose where his family would settle. Once the family had land, the father had a great deal of physical work to do. He had to clear the land of trees and **underbrush** so that the family could begin farming. Clearing the land was very difficult. The father and sons spent long hours using axes to chop down trees. They used the trees that were cut down to build a house and a barn.

In forested areas, settlers had to cut down hundreds of trees and remove the stumps before they could begin farming the land.

Fishing was a way for pioneer men to relax with friends while also getting food for their families.

Once the land was cleared, the father spent most of his time farming. He fed the farm animals. He planted and **harvested** crops. When he was not farming, he spent time hunting and fishing to provide food for his family.

Did you know:

Most pioneer fathers made all the furniture in their family's home.

First-hand account:

In this account, a pioneer remembers how hard his father worked at clearing the land.

In the bush it was cut, cut, chop, chop, all day long... I can remember my dad coming in to the shack at night and he'd say, "It's hard, Mother, it's hard." That's all he ever said. All day for Dad it was chop, chop, chop. Down, up, down, up. It never ended. He got strong though. Those wrestlers on television are flabby compared to him. Muscles that stood out. He certainly felt healthy.

A Mother's Work

A pioneer wife worked just as hard as her husband. Pioneer women had many responsibilities on Canada's early homesteads. They spent long hours tending to their family's basic needs. Pioneer women prepared all the meals, cleaned the home, and cared for the children. They also made clothing and blankets for the family. This meant that the mother worked at weaving cloth, spinning yarn, and sewing and mending.

In addition to doing all the household chores, pioneer women worked very hard on the farm. They helped clear the land and plant and harvest the crops. On many pioneer farms, the women took care of the chickens. They also grew vegetables in small gardens near the home. Most of these vegetables were grown to feed the family.

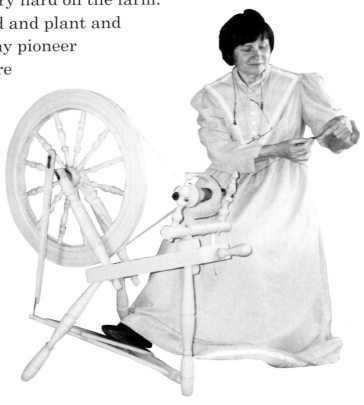

Pioneer women spun wool from sheep into yarn that could be used to knit socks, mittens, and sweaters.

Pioneer women often looked after the family's cows. Women fed and milked the cows, and made the milk into butter.

Did you know:

Early families in Canada made their own cloth. The family sheared sheep and then the mother spun the wool into yarn. Flax was also grown, then spun into thread and made into linen.

First-hand account:

In this account, a pioneer remembers how good her mother was to the rest of her family.

[Our house] was made of logs and roofed with turf or sod, which is . . . inadequate in the rain. I never realized until I grew up what a lot my mother had to put up with, but I know on wet nights she had to sit up and hold umbrellas over us to keep us warm, and when she got her own sleep those nights, goodness knows.

Children's Chores

Pioneer families in early Canada were very big. Some families had as many as sixteen children! All the children, except for the babies and toddlers, had chores to do every day. This meant that there was very little time for playing. Often, the boys helped their father on the farm. Older boys helped clear the land, plough the fields, and harvest the crops. They also helped build furniture, hunt, and fish. The younger boys helped herd cattle and tend to the crops. They also gathered firewood.

Young boys learned to plough fields. This skill helped them when they grew up and started their own farms.

Did you know:

Besides chores, older children were expected to do schoolwork. If there was a schoolhouse nearby, the children might attend school there. However, in many families, it was up to the mother to teach her children how to read and write.

Washing clothes was difficult for pioneer women. Clothes had to be scrubbed, wrung out, and hung on a clothesline to dry.

Most girls in pioneer families helped their mothers with household chores. The older girls spun wool and helped with the sewing. They also helped their mother prepare food. They **churned** butter and gathered eggs. Little girls learned how to knit at an early age. They also fed the chickens and set the table at mealtime. All the girls in the family helped their mother with the washing. Sharing the household and farm chores helped the children to learn the skills they would need as adults.

First-hand account:

In this account, an old man remembers his childhood days on a pioneer farm.

One sure thing about those days, we sure knew how to work. It wasn't exactly that we called it work, it was more like just part of our lives. If I'm not mistaken, I couldn't have been more than six when I put my childhood things away...Even before five or six, though, we were doing things around the yard, hunting up broody hens and getting them back to the henhouse, going for the cows with Spot, our collie, and handing my dad things when he was fixing a piece of machinery.

Tools of the Family Home

Pioneer families did not have modern tools to make their lives easier. There were no microwaves, vacuum cleaners, or tractors to help them with their chores. Instead, settlers had useful, simple tools. For example, children made candles so that the family could have light when the sun went down. Following are other important tools that helped pioneer families in early Canada.

The Fireplace

The fireplace was one of the most important tools in the early Canadian home. Usually the fireplace was made of stone. It stood in the kitchen, if there was one, and had a large chimney. Pioneer families used the fireplace for cooking and to stay warm. Cooking pots hung above the fire on metal rods. An iron rack inside the fireplace held burning logs. In the winter, the fireplace was the only source of heat in the home. Because of this, the family had to make sure the fire never went out. If the fire did go out, it would be very difficult to start it again.

Carding Paddles and Spinning Wheels

Many early Canadian families made their own clothes. In the early 1800s, wool was one of the most common materials for clothing. It kept the family warm in the harsh Canadian weather. To make wool into yarn, pioneers had to use carding paddles and a spinning wheel. The pioneers used carding paddles to pull the wool apart and clean off excess dirt. The spinning wheel was then used to turn these bits of wool into yarn. The wheel twisted wool while the **spinner** pulled it to the proper thickness.

Farming Tools

At first, pioneer families only had basic tools. An axe was used to chop down trees and trim logs. A hoe and spade were used for digging. A plough pulled by horses or oxen was used to cut through the soil and turn it over. A tool called a scythe was used to cut grain or hay. A scythe consists of a long, slightly curved blade on a long stick. Some farmers used a sickle to cut grain as well. A sickle is a short, curved blade on a short stick. Most of the early farming tools on Canadian farms were handmade. By the mid-1800s, farmers could buy new, **mass-produced** tools that made farming easier.

A Year in the Life

Pioneer families worked hard all year. The family had to complete daily tasks such as cooking, cleaning, and feeding farm animals. They also had special jobs for different times of the year. Each season brought a new set of chores to parents and children. Here is a look at how many families in early Canada spent their farming seasons.

Spring

Spring marked the beginning of a new farming season. As soon as the snow disappeared and the ground was dry, farming activities began. The men in the family spent the spring ploughing fields and planting new crops. The women helped the men plant the crops. The women also planted the vegetables in the garden. Everyone in the family worked to make sure that their farm would be productive in the coming months.

Summer

In the late summer, the family spent time cutting and drying hay. This task was long and tiring, but it was important. The family needed to make sure that they would have enough hay to feed the horses and other farm animals for the rest of the year. Cutting hay was not the only summer chore. Women and girls tended to the garden and the house. Men and boys took care of the farm animals and hunted and fished for food. The summer days were long, so the family worked in daylight.

Autumn

Autumn was the busiest season of the year for a pioneer family. This is because autumn was harvest time. The family needed to harvest their wheat and other crops so that they would have food to eat over the winter. Everyone helped with the harvesting. The men walked through the wheat fields winging their scythes or sickles. As the men cut the wheat, the women followed behind them. The women tied the stalks of cut grain into bundles called sheaves. After the wheat and other crops were harvested, the family worked together to prepare the crops for the coming winter. The women **preserved** the crops from the field and garden. The men **threshed** the wheat so the family would have flour for the rest of the year.

Winter

The winter months were very cold in most parts of Canada. As a result, activity on the farm was less hectic for most pioneer families. The men of the pioneer families spent much of the winter repairing tools, making furniture, and cutting wood. They needed to ensure that there was plenty of firewood to keep the family warm. In the winter, the women of the family kept busy mending old clothes and making new clothes. They also caught up on chores that had been ignored during the busy autumn season. Winter was a favourite time of year for pioneer children. Since there was less work to be done in the winter, the children could spend a little time having fun. They enjoyed outdoor activities such as tobogganing, ice-skating, and snowball fights.

Loneliness and Working Bees

Life in early Canada could be quite lonely for pioneer families. When families settled in Canada, they often left grandparents, aunts, uncles, and cousins back in their **homelands**. To keep in touch, pioneer families wrote letters to their relatives. They wrote about their adventures and hardships.

In Canada's early days, farms were usually far apart from each other and from villages. At first, families had few neighbours. As more neighbours arrived in the area, they made an effort to see each other. Sometimes they gathered to help each other with large tasks. They worked together to build new houses, **husk** corn, and chop trees. These work gatherings were called **bees**. Adults and older children took part in the working bees while younger children played nearby. After the work was done, everyone enjoyed dinner, music, and dancing. Work that would take one family months would be done by many people in one day.

Did you know:

Working bees were social events for families. A host family spent a lot of time preparing meals for the neighbours who were coming to help them.

Working bees helped pioneers build communities. They built homes, barns, and friendships that lasted for many years.

First-hand account:

Catharine Parr Trail was a well-known pioneer in Canada. She wrote many books and articles about life in the wilderness. Here, she remembers the working bee that was called to help build a house for her and her husband.

It was the end of October and the outside walls of our house were not yet up. We decided to call a bee. Sixteen of our neighbours answered our call. Even though the weather was not good, our "hive" worked so hard that by night the walls were raised. The work went on merrily…huge joints of salt pork, a peck of potatoes, with rice pudding and a [huge] loaf [of bread] formed the feast for them during the raising.

Pioneer Fun

In Canada's early days, settlers had little time for fun. Pioneer families turned their work into fun. One way they did this was by taking part in bees. Children often played games during their chores to make them seem like fun. Young girls raced to see who could card wool faster. Boys had contests to see who could carry the most wood.

Once the day's chores were done, the whole family gathered around the fireplace. They spent time in the evenings reading and telling stories. Sometimes fathers sat by the fire and **whittled** wood into toys for the younger children. Most toys in pioneer families were homemade. Children spent many winter evenings playing games like homemade wooden jacks or checkers. In the summer, they played games outside like marbles or hide and seek. Parents also found time to visit with friends and attend parties and dances.

Children turned many chores into fun games. Fetching wood for the stove could be turned into a fun ride.

First-hand account:

In this account, a pioneer remembers wanting a doll when she was a little girl. Many pioneer girls owned homemade dolls.

For one of my birthdays I remember I wanted a doll. Mother... made me a ragdoll. Having visions of a lovely china-faced one with curls, I was so hurt I threw [my ragdoll] into the pigsty... I know Mother must have shed some tears at my ungratefulness. I never remember owning a real doll....

Did you know:

As years passed on the pioneer farm, things became easier for the family. Once the farm was producing plenty of crops, the family was able to build a larger home and enjoy more free time.

Family Life Past and Present

Family life in early Canada was very different from family life today. Today's children do not have nearly as many chores as Canadian pioneer children did. Children today are not expected to rise before sunset to feed the farm animals or bring wood inside for the fire. Fathers no longer have to make furniture for the house, and mothers no longer have to use a spinning wheel. Today, families have more spare time, but everyone still has chores to do.

Chores

Which of the chores below would apply to families today and families from the past? Which chores would apply only to families in early Canada?

Make your bed before breakfast.

Bring the firewood inside.

Help preserve fruits, vegetables, and meat for the winter.

Help with the washing and cooking.

Cut hay for the farm animals.

Today's families do not have to work as hard as pioneer families. Families today have more free time for fun activities such as picnics.

Early Families

- Very large families, up to sixteen children
- Families worked at chores from sunrise to sunset
- Some pioneer families lived in one-room cabins or shacks
- Most families farmed
- A large fireplace heated the family home
- Pioneers families often made their own clothing and furniture

Then

- Children are expected to do schoolwork
- Winter is a time for families to enjoy outdoor activities
- Boys and girls help their parents with chores

Now

Today's Families

- Smaller families, usually two to four children
- No one is expected to work from sunrise to sunset
- Live in homes with more than one room
- Most families today do not farm
- Homes are heated with modern heaters
- Families get their food, clothing, and furniture from stores

DIAGRAM

There are many differences between today's families and those of long ago. There are also similarities. The diagram on the left compares these differences and similarities. Copy the diagram in your notebook. Try to think of other similarities and differences to add to your diagram.

As you can see by the diagram, you and your family have some things in common with families who lived in Canada more than 100 years ago.

Preserving the Past

Pioneer families came from near and far to live in Canada's unsettled regions. Some left their homes in England, France, Germany, Scotland, and other countries in Europe to settle in Canada. Others left the United States to live farther north. Still others moved from eastern Canada to western Canada. The pioneers travelled great distances to settle on unfamiliar land. They travelled by boat and by wagon until they found a piece of land on which to settle and start a new life. The map on the next page shows which parts of Canada the pioneer families settled, and when they arrived.

Loyalist settlers in the Maritimes

1. Pioneers first arrived in New France, present-day Quebec, in the seventeenth and eighteenth centuries.

2. Pioneer families settled in the Maritimes and Upper Canada from 1760 to 1860.

3. Families settled throughout the Canadian prairies from 1870 to 1914.

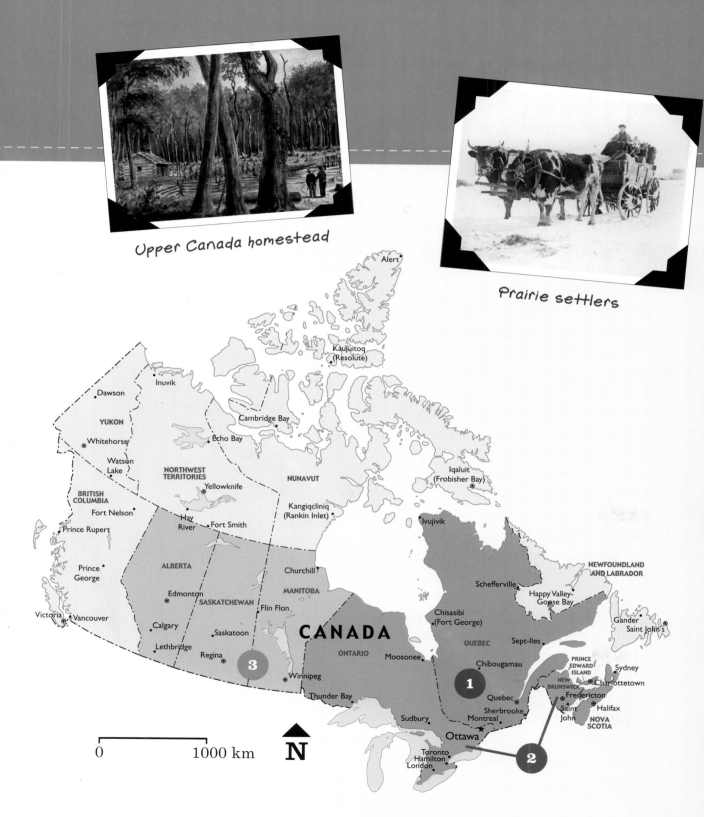

Upper Canada homestead

Prairie settlers

Alert

Kaujuitoq
(Resolute)

Inuvik

Dawson

YUKON

Cambridge Bay

Whitehorse

Echo Bay

Watson
Lake

**NORTHWEST
TERRITORIES**

NUNAVUT

Iqaluit
(Frobisher Bay)

**BRITISH
COLUMBIA**

Yellowknife

Fort Nelson

Kangiqcliniq
(Rankin Inlet)

Ivujivik

Hay
River

Fort Smith

Prince Rupert

**NEWFOUNDLAND
AND LABRADOR**

Prince
George

ALBERTA

Churchill

Schefferville

Happy Valley-
Goose Bay

Edmonton

MANITOBA

Victoria

Vancouver

SASKATCHEWAN

Flin Flon

CANADA

Chisasibi
(Fort George)

Gander
Saint John's

Calgary

Saskatoon

Sept-Iles

QUEBEC

Lethbridge

Regina

3

ONTARIO

Moosonee

Chibougamau

**PRINCE
EDWARD
ISLAND**

Sydney

Winnipeg

1

Quebec

**NEW
BRUNSWICK**

Charlottetown

Fredericton

Thunder Bay

Sherbrooke

Saint
John

Halifax

Sudbury

Montreal

2

**NOVA
SCOTIA**

Ottawa

Toronto
Hamilton
London

0   1000 km   **N**

23

Glossary

Bees: social gatherings held to perform a task

Churned: stirred up quickly to make butter

Harvested: collected crops

Homelands: the lands where people are from

Homestead: a parcel of land in the Canadian West granted to a settler by the government

Husk: to remove the external covering of corn and other fruits and vegetables

Mass-produced: made in large quantities

Preserved: preparing food so that it will not go bad

Spinner: the person who operates the spinning wheel

Threshed: separating the grain or seeds from wheat

Underbrush: shrubs and vines that grow under large trees in the woods

Whittled: cut, trimmed, and carved with a knife

Index